AI in Telecommunications

Enhancing the Network and Connectivity

Table of Contents

Chapter 1. Introduction

In this Special Report, we delve into a highly intriguing and technically complex intersection: Artificial Intelligence (AI) in Telecommunications. As our world becomes increasingly interconnected, the reliability and efficiency of telecom networks are paramount, and AI has emerged as a crucial facilitator in enhancing these aspects. From smart routing to predictive maintenance, from personalized customer service to network optimization, AI is pushing telecommunications into a dynamic new era. Though this topic entails intricate technological synergies, rest assured, the report breaks it down in an easy-to-understand, conservative, down-to-earth manner. We steer clear of unnecessary jargon to ensure it's not just the tech savvy that benefit but everyone with a curiosity for how AI is revolutionizing telecommunications. This special report will serve as your compass, guiding you through the complex but fascinating labyrinth of AI's role in the telecom industry.

Chapter 2. Understanding the AI and Telecommunications Nexus

The advent of Artificial Intelligence (AI) technology has disseminated into various industries, exerting a transformative impact. Similarly, the telecommunications sector is no exception. The potential of AI to refine and revolutionize multiple facets of this industry, from network operations and customer experience to revenue creation, implores a closer examination. This review will elucidate the interplay between AI and the telecommunications industry, its applications, benefits, and the future outlook.

2.1. Understanding Artificial Intelligence in Telecommunications

AI, with its dynamic algorithms and advanced computing abilities, provides ample opportunities to overcome the traditional challenges faced by telecom operators. Here, AI is not simply another piece of technology, but essentially, a potent catalyst predicted to fully transform the way telecommunications industry operates.

In telecom networks, AI extends its role beyond digitization, emphasizing intelligent automation. This implies that with AI, operations are not just automated, but they 'learn' and 'improve' over time, enhancing their efficacy and reliability. Over the years, telecom operators have amassed extensive volumes of data — a significant portion of it unanalysed. AI techniques such as machine learning (ML), help in analysing this data to uncover hidden patterns, which can prove beneficial in various operational dimensions such as network planning, optimization, predicting client behavior, and more.

2.2. AI Applications in Telecommunications

AI's diverse range of applications in telecommunications can be broadly categorized into network operations, user experience, and revenue creation. Each category elucidates how AI has the potential to re-architect the telecommunications sector.

2.3. Network Operations

AI can significantly reduce the complexity of network operations as it helps monitor, manage and optimize the networks. By applying predictive analytics, AI can foresee potential network issues and take counteractive measures even before the problem exacerbates, enhancing the network's overall reliability.

Also, AI can perform predictive maintenance by analyzing various parameters like signal strength, network load, and device history. Through real-time monitoring, AI can predict a likely equipment failure and schedule maintenance, reducing unexpectedly high downtime and enhancing customer satisfaction.

2.4. User Experience

AI significantly enhances the user experience by driving personalized customer interactions. Advanced AI algorithms are capable of profiling customers, understanding their needs, and consequently, providing highly customized solutions. AI-driven chatbots and virtual assistants are capable of resolving customer queries promptly, enhancing customer satisfaction and alleviating strain on customer service representatives.

Moreover, utilizing AI for fraud detection enhances user trust and safety. AI algorithms can identify abnormal user behavior, flagging potential fraud cases to be investigated further.

2.5. Revenue Creation

AI also opens up new revenue streams in telecom. Predictive analytics provided by AI enables companies to understand the customer's behaviour, identify their needs, and offer valuable services and products accordingly. Moreover, AI-powered recommendation engines can suggest additional services to the customers based on their preferences and usage patterns.

In fact, with the advent of 5G, the role of AI in revenue creation will become even more prominent. The high-speed data transfer capability of 5G can be leveraged by AI to make real-time decisions, offering numerous new services and thus, amplifying revenues.

2.6. Looking Ahead: The Future of AI in Telecommunications

Looking ahead, the role of AI in telecommunications will continue to expand. The integration of AI with other emerging technologies like the Internet of Things (IoT), blockchain, and edge computing will further revolutionize the telecom industry.

Moreover, the advent of 5G technology will further refine the potential of AI, allowing telecom companies to offer new services such as remote surgeries, autonomous driving, and more. By predicting network congestion and dynamically managing workloads, AI will ensure that critical applications run processing smoothly no matter how congested the network is.

But the journey is not without challenges. Telecom companies will need to invest in AI talent and infrastructure, while also addressing regulatory, data privacy, and ethical issues. However, with the potential returns that AI offers, these challenges seem surmountable.

It is evident from the above that AI and telecommunications share a critical symbiosis. With the right progression, their fusion heralds not just an easing of operational challenges, but also a radical reconstitution of how the entire telecom industry functions. Therefore, understanding and investing in this nexus can prove to be a genesis for telecom service providers in the age of digital transformation. AI, thus, sits at the heart of a paradigm shift in the telecommunications industry.

Chapter 3. AI's Role in Network Optimization

Today, network optimization practices are at the heart of ensuring robust connectivity, low latency, and overall efficient communication infrastructure. Significantly, AI is playing more than just a supportive role in achieving these objectives. Leveraging the power of machine learning algorithms combined with advanced data analytics techniques, AI is transforming the way telecom operators optimize their networks.

3.1. The Significance of Network Optimization

Network optimization is essentially the fine-tuning of a network to ensure it is performing at its best. Multiple factors make up network optimization including planning, design, setup, and management. For telecom network operators, optimized networks mean more efficient and reliable operations, elevated customer experience, reduced operational costs and increased profitability.

AI has revolutionized the way telecom operators approach network optimization. Instead of a reactive maintenance mode, AI enables a proactive approach that not only recognizes but also predicts and resolves issues before they escalate.

3.2. Application of AI in Network Optimization

AI is touching every facet of network optimization within the telecommunications industry. Let's explore some of the significant applications:

1. **Traffic prediction and management:** Telecom operators use AI to forecast network traffic based on past data and trends. Once predicted, the system can adjust infrastructural resources like microwave link capacities and virtual machines, effectively managing the traffic loads and reducing latency.

2. **Resource allocation:** AI can dynamically adjust resource allocation based on real-time network conditions, allocation and usage of infrastructure. AI's predictive ability further enhances this by proactively allocating resources based on anticipated demand.

3. **Overall Equipment Efficiency (OEE):** AI has the capability to run insights and predict trends on key parameters to improve the Overall Equipment Efficiency (OEE), boost network uptime and reduce overall costs.

3.3. AI-Driven Predictive Maintenance

One of the key aspects where AI has a definitive impact is predictive maintenance. By analyzing historical data for correlations and patterns that indicate a potential equipment failure, AI can predict when maintenance will be required, allowing telecom operators to take preventive action minimizing disruptions.

AI's ability to analyze vast amounts of data can also help identify irregularities swiftly, contributing to faster problem resolution. This proactive approach not only improves customer satisfaction but significantly reduces network downtime and maintenance costs, thus driving revenue.

3.4. Enhancing Connectivity with Self-Organizing Networks (SON)

Self-Organizing Networks (SON) is a powerful manifestation of AI in telecommunications. They incorporate real-time response capabilities of a neural network with the learning capabilities of machine learning to configure, optimize, and heal telecom networks automatically.

SONs can adjust to varied scenarios such as shifts in traffic patterns, equipment failure, or interference, improving the performance and reliability of networks. AI's role lies in 'teaching' the network to make these adjustments, using machine learning algorithms to learn from historical datasets and predict behavioral patterns.

3.5. The Challenge of Network Security

As telecom networks expand and become increasingly complex, they also become more vulnerable to security threats. AI steps in here as a game-changer. With its ability to analyze high volumes of data in real-time, AI can identify and alert about security threats before they escalate, enhancing the overall security of telecom networks.

AI-based systems can monitor abnormal network behavior, recognize patterns, and introduce countermeasures, hence, acting as a robust protective layer.

3.6. Conclusion – The Future of AI in Network Optimization

AI-driven network optimization is rapidly becoming the new norm for telecommunications. Learning capabilities, predictive algorithms, and real-time data analysis make AI a potent tool to optimize network efficiency, bolster security, and enhance customer experience.

With continuing advances in AI and machine learning, there's potential for more radical changes. The future will witness AI-powered networks self-diagnosing problems, initiating preventive measures, and even self-healing to ensure consistent and top-notch service quality. AI will intimately intertwine with telecommunications, building an agile, robust, and optimized network that can cater to the ever-evolving needs of the digital era. So, while we may have just begun to scratch the surface of what AI can offer, it's clear that its impact on telecom network optimization is transformative and here to stay.

Chapter 4. Predictive Maintenance: AI's Proactive Approach

Artificial Intelligence (AI) is increasingly permeating every aspect of the telecommunications industry, and predictive maintenance, in particular, represents an area where AI innovation has seen significant uptakes. This approach leverages data to predict and prevent system failures, optimize maintenance schedules, reduce costs, and thereby improve system reliability and performance overall.

4.1. Background: Understanding the Need for Predictive Maintenance

Predictive maintenance in the world of telecom isn't a new idea, but the application of AI technologies has given it a fresh perspective. To understand its significance, let's travel back a few decades. Telecommunication systems, such as switching systems and transmission lines, were built using technology that was designed to last, but that could still fail. When failure occurred, the consequences were often significant: from customer dissatisfaction due to disrupted services, to substantial financial losses.

Traditional maintenance methods, i.e., reactive and preventative maintenance, have been standard for years. Reactive maintenance refers to fixing things when they break, while preventative maintenance involves routine checks to mitigate the risk of sudden failures. While these methods have served networks reasonably well in the past, they possess a considerable number of downsides.

Reactive maintenance can lead to unexpected downtime and

disruption to services, causing customer dissatisfaction. Preventative maintenance, on the other hand, can be expensive and time-consuming, often involving unnecessary checks on components that are still operational and not close to failing.

This sets the stage for predictive maintenance, an approach that offers the potential to improve the efficiency of maintenance procedures, reduce costs, and improve the reliability of telecommunication networks.

4.2. The Rise of AI & Machine Learning in Predictive Maintenance

Predictive maintenance utilizes AI and Machine Learning (ML) technologies to analyze vast amounts of data gathered from various network components. This data can include historical failure rates, real-time performance data, and external factors, such as weather conditions, that can affect component performance. The overall aim is to predict future component failure before it occurs, thereby allowing for proactive maintenance.

Machine Learning, a subset of AI, plays a particularly important role here. Algorithms are used to sift through the gathered data, learning from it, recognizing patterns, and identifying signs that might point to a potential failure. This process of learning improves the accuracy of predictions over time, resulting in more efficient and effective maintenance schedules.

AI further augments this approach by providing intelligent insights from the data. Such insights could be highlighting a potential weakness in a component that has not failed yet but might do so soon, recommending action based on historical data, or comparing performance of similar network components to identify abnormal behavior.

4.3. The Components of AI-Driven Predictive Maintenance

An AI-driven predictive maintenance approach is based on several key components, including:

- Data Collection: This involves gathering information from various sources including network logs, sensor outputs, historical maintenance records, and even external factors such as weather data.

- Data Processing: The acquired data, often vast and unstructured, is processed and cleaned, eliminating noise and preparing it for analysis.

- Feature Extraction: Key features that impact network performance are identified and extracted for further analysis.

- Model Development: Machine Learning models are trained using the processed data. These models learn from the features and the corresponding network performance, allowing them to predict future performance based on new data.

- Predictive Analysis: The trained models are then implemented to forecast future failure events based on real-time data.

- Actionable Insights: Based on the prediction output and the criticality of anticipated failures, maintenance actions are recommended.

4.4. Real-World Applications and Case Studies

Adoption of AI for predictive maintenance in the telecom sector is becoming more common. For example, major telecom providers have turned to AI to predict failures in optical networks. Companies have successfully trained Machine Learning models to predict failures in network components up to seven days before they actually occur. In another instance, AI models have been used on individual cell towers to predict components that might fail within the next 48 hours, with an impressive 95% accuracy.

Not only does this allow network operators to deploy maintenance teams more effectively, but it also reduces overall system downtime, leading to improved customer experiences and cost savings.

4.5. The Future of Predictive Maintenance: Opportunities and Challenges

The future of predictive maintenance in telecommunication networks looks promising, albeit with a few hurdles.

On the bright side, new technologies, such as IoT (Internet of Things) and 5G, present exciting opportunities. IoT devices, with their capability of real-time data collection and communication, make excellent data sources for predictive maintenance. Similarly, the implementation of 5G technology will result in denser networks, offering more data for AI models to draw valuable predictions from.

However, accompanying these opportunities, challenges lurk as well. Issues of data privacy, security, and the management of vast volumes of data are key concerns. The ability to ensure a high quality of data and the challenge of processing and managing it efficiently will test future predictive maintenance systems.

Despite these hurdles, with the benefits offered by AI-driven predictive maintenance, there is significant motivation to overcome these challenges and unlock the compelling potential of this technology in the telecom sector. The journey ahead is certainly exciting, laden with innovations that will reshape telecom maintenance strategies as we know them.

Chapter 5. Smart Routing in Telecom: AI's Masterstroke

Telecommunication networks are largely responsible for the flow of information around the globe. One of the key processes within this intricate system is the routing of data packets from their source to their destination. With the deployment of AI, this integral task has been significantly streamlined. Known as 'Smart Routing', this AI-driven method enables enhanced network efficiency, lower latency and improved reliability.

5.1. Understanding the Basics

In traditional routing methods, data packets would follow a pre-determined route from their source to their destination. This singular trajectory did not consider variations in network conditions. This static approach could result in sub-optimal use of network resources, and could lead to network congestion during peak data usage periods.

In contrast, smart routing has brought about a paradigm shift in this process. AI algorithms analyze the network's condition in real-time and choose the most efficient path for each data packet. By comparing data on network congestion, latency, and packet loss, the algorithm can navigate the packet through the most effective route at any given moment.

5.2. Key Influences of AI on Smart Routing

The real magic is woven by AI's ability to learn and adapt. AI-based decision machines deployed in smart routing grow more efficient over time. They continuously learn and adapt from the network conditions, user behaviors, and from their successes and failures, facilitating constant system improvement.

This capability has two primary impacts on smart routing:

Dynamic Routing: Unlike traditional systems which follow a predetermined route, smart routing allows for dynamic changes, responsive to real-time network conditions. This is critical in ensuring uninterrupted, high-speed data flow, especially during peak data usage periods.

Predictive Analysis: AI's capability to learn allows it to deliver predictive analysis regarding future network conditions. The system can preemptively maneuver data through routes predicted to have lower congestion in the future, thus further increasing overall network efficiency.

5.3. The Impact on Network Latency and Reliability

Network latency refers to the delay incurred when data moves from its source to the destination. Higher latency can hamper real-time communications, rendering services such as Voice over Internet Protocol (VoIP) and online gaming ineffective. The dynamic nature of smart routing helps reduce network latency by ensuring data packets always take the path with the least resistance.

In the same vein, reliability refers to the ability to deliver data packets from their source to destination without loss. Data packet loss can result in poorer quality of service. Smart routing improves service reliability by finding and utilizing the best paths for data transmission and diverting data from paths with a higher likelihood of packet loss.

5.4. Commercial Implications of AI-Driven Smart Routing

Apart from enhancing network efficiency, latency, and reliability, AI-powered smart routing holds significant commercial potential.

Customer Retention: By providing a seamless and high-quality connection, telecom firms stand a better chance at customer satisfaction and retention, which is crucial in today's competitive market.

Optimized Resource usage: By diverting traffic away from heavily loaded network paths, AI-backed smart routers ensure a more balanced, and thus optimized, use of network resources.

Real-time Troubleshooting: The AI systems in smart routing not only streamline data flow but also monitor networks for any irregularities. They can spot potential issues, alert network teams, and often address the problem autonomously.

5.5. The Road Ahead

The potential of AI in smart routing is far from fully realized. As AI technologies mature, we can expect the evolution of smarter, more adaptable, and scalable telecommunication networks. These networks will provide superior quality services, manage ever-growing data traffic gracefully, and offer commercially viable optimizations.

While the complexities of AI-driven smart routing may seem intimidating, the pragmatic applicability of this technology cannot be ignored. Its successful deployment catapults communication networks from static, rule-bound systems into dynamic, adaptable lifelines of global connectivity, reinforcing and enhancing the critical role telecommunications play in our increasingly interconnected world.

Chapter 6. The Personalization Spectrum with AI in Customer Service

Telecommunications providers operate in a highly competitive environment, where top-notch customer service is a critical differentiator. With millions of users worldwide engaging with various communication services daily, personalizing the customer experience (CX) can provide a unique value proposition to customers while simultaneously reducing operating costs. AI's capabilities – including machine learning (ML), natural language processing (NLP), and predictive analytics – promise transformative outcomes and are fundamentally changing how telecommunications providers interact with their customers.

6.1. The Role of AI in Personalization

The growing demand for personalization, coupled with the explosion of available customer data, presents lucrative opportunities and profound challenges for telecom providers. Customers expect omnichannel experiences that are highly personalized while also adhering to strict privacy guidelines. Conventional systems and manual processes cannot meet these demands. Here is where AI comes into the picture.

AI leverages machine learning algorithms to decipher patterns, trends, and customer preferences from large datasets. With the predictive capabilities of AI, telecom companies can offer personalized communication services based on various customer attributes such as age, location, lifestyle, and browsing habits.

In addition to personalization, AI can aid in real-time decision-making, driving proactive engagement, and fostering customer loyalty. It does this by predicting customer behavior, offering relevant recommendations, and optimizing customer interactions on various touchpoints such as call centers, websites, social media, and customer self-service portals.

6.2. AI and Customer Segmentation

One of the fundamental applications of AI in customer service personalization is segmenting customers into distinct groups. Before the advent of AI, segmentation was primarily based on demographic data or other broad categories, which often led to generic customer profiles.

With AI, telecom companies can now perform granular segmentation based on individual customer preferences and behavior. For instance, AI can analyze a single customer's call history, data usage, top-up frequency, browsing habits, and more. The result is a comprehensive, single-customer view that enables personalized communication and offers tailored to individual needs.

6.3. Enhancing Customer Journey with AI

Personalization plays an instrumental role in shaping the customer journey. AI enables telecom operators to map out each customer's journey, from new activations to device upgrades to seeking support. With AI, telecom companies can personalize each stage of this journey, driving better customer satisfaction and enhancing lifetime value.

Telecom companies can use AI to send personalized notifications about network issues to impacted customers, suggest the optimal time for device upgrades, or even guide customers through their self-service journey. This proactive approach not only improves customer satisfaction, but it also helps preempt potential issues that could negatively impact the relationship.

6.4. Using AI for Predictive Personalization

In today's data-rich environment, customers expect their telecom providers to anticipate their needs and make relevant offers. AI's predictive analytics capabilities allow telecom companies to analyze existing customer data and predict future behaviors, preferences, and needs.

For example, by analyzing data usage patterns, telecom companies can predict when a user is likely to deplete their data package and send proactive alerts or tailored data top-up options. Predictive personalization reduces churn by ensuring customers always feel valued and understood, reinforcing a positive feedback loop in the customer-telecom provider relationship.

6.5. NLP for Personalized Customer Interactions

Natural Language Processing (NLP), a subfield of AI that involves human-computer interaction, is revolutionizing customer service. NLP can understand, analyze, and generate human language in a valuable way. For telecom companies, this means being able to automate and personalize customer interactions like never before.

AI chatbots powered by NLP can provide intelligent and personalized responses to customer queries, offering 24/7 support. They can parse and understand customer requests in natural language, respond, and even learn from these interactions to improve future responses. This significantly enhances customer satisfaction as users receive quick, efficient, and personalized service.

6.6. Ethical Considerations in AI-driven Personalization

Despite its clear benefits, AI-driven personalization in telecommunications raises some ethical considerations. Telecom providers face the critical task of ensuring privacy, security, and fairness while leveraging AI for personalization.

The misuse of collected personal data can result in an infringement of privacy. AI systems must be designed with stringent privacy measures in line with regulations like the General Data Protection Regulation (GDPR). Furthermore, telecom providers need to ensure that AI systems do not unintentionally create or perpetuate biases which may compromise fair service delivery.

6.7. The Future of Customer Service

In conclusion, AI holds tremendous potential in telecom. It can provide high-quality and cost-effective customer service, predict consumer trends, and streamline business processes. The scale of these benefits dramatically increases when AI is used to deliver personalized customer experiences.

Nevertheless, the road to full AI adoption in telecommunications customer service is not without challenges, including ensuring data security and privacy, and identifying and addressing potential AI biases. Success will hinge on telecom providers' ability to strike the right balance between using AI to deliver personalized services, while also maintaining the trust and confidence of their customers.

Chapter 7. Case Studies: Successful AI Implementations in Telecommunications

The inroads made by AI in the telecommunications sector are many-fold, and the below case studies exemplify its successful implementation. These examples illustrate how AI is driving advancements, improving efficiencies, and paving the way for future developments.

7.1. AI-Powered Predictive Maintenance: AT&T Case

AT&T, one of the world's largest telecommunications companies, has integrated AI into its day-to-day functioning and strategic planning. One area where AT&T has successfully used AI is in predictive maintenance of its network infrastructure.

AT&T's data-driven infrastructure handles enormous amounts of data, a fact that necessitates constant monitoring for abnormalities. Recognizing this, AT&T employs AI algorithms to predict and prevent potential issues before they occur. Machine Learning models are trained on past network data, enabling them to analyze patterns and anomalies in real-time, thus predicting potential equipment failures or service disruptions ahead of time.

Resultantly, AT&T can proactively address equipment malfunctions. This enhances network reliability, minimizes unforeseen costs, and improves customer satisfaction by preventing outages or service disruptions.

7.2. Smart Routing: Telefonica Case

Telefonica, a leading telecom company in Spain, employed AI to resolve issues in traffic routing. The company's operations span across numerous countries and various demographic segments, each with individual network preferences and workloads.

Telefonica implemented AI-based neural networks to optimize its traffic routing. These networks analyze vast amounts of data, learn from historical logs and real-time network statuses, then make instant decisions about the ideal route for data transmission.

AI application allowed Telefonica to efficiently manage network traffic during peak and off-peak hours, reducing lags and improving the customer experience. It also helped Telefonica reduce its energy footprint by intelligently managing its network load and avoiding unnecessary energy expenditure.

7.3. Customer Service Personalization: Vodafone Case

Vodafone turned to AI solutions to enhance its customer service deliveries. They introduced an AI-powered chatbot, TOBi, to streamline customer interactions.

TOBi, equipped with Natural Language Processing capabilities, interacts with customers in real-time, capably understanding and responding to inquiries. The AI can recognize the context of the conversation, retrieve relevant information, and provide effective solutions. TOBi can also transact sales, executing customer purchases and handling billing inquiries, significantly reducing time spent by customers in queues.

Vodafone's AI initiative streamlined customer interactions and drastically reduced waiting times, leading to improved customer satisfaction rates.

7.4. Network Optimization: Verizon Case

Verizon implemented an AI-based solution to optimize their communication network. The telecom giant created predictive models that could analyze multitudes of network variables, enabling them to anticipate future needs.

These models use machine learning algorithms which continually learn and adapt to changes in network behavior. Consequently, Verizon gained an intricate understanding of its network's functionality, including recognizing patterns signifying potential congestions or disruptions.

Resultantly, Verizon could manipulate network parameters efficiently, ensuring optimal service even during anticipated high-usage events. The ability to predict and prevent potential service disruptions significantly enhanced Verizon's reliability and competitiveness in the industry.

Through these case studies, it is evident that AI presents diverse potentialities within the telecom sector. Whether in the realm of maintenance, routing, customer service, or network optimization, AI has played a transformative role. As these technologies continue to evolve, we will only further unravel AI's vast potential within the telecommunications industry. By embracing AI, telecommunications companies can steer their course toward a future of constantly evolving innovation, enhanced efficiency, and exceptional user experience.

Chapter 8. Challenges and Obstacles in AI Adoption

Before we delve into solutions that AI promises for the future of telecommunications, it's essential to consider the hurdles that must be surmounted before reaching this utopian vision. The following topics, addressed in depth, represent the key challenges which impede the widespread adoption of AI technologies in the telecom sector.

8.1. Understanding the Complexity of AI

AI is not an easy subject to grasp, particularly for people without a background in technology. The technical intricacies make it a hard sell to stakeholders who are not well-versed in the field. This challenge extends to a broader curriculum issue within the telecommunications sector. To fully incorporate AI within their operations, firms must foster a working culture comfortable with AI and its associated technologies. Training and education programs, starting at executive levels and permeating through the telecoms workforce, will be a critical measure to ensure a successful AI transition.

Discussions about AI often veer into esoteric territories or become mired in complexities that make comprehension difficult for the uninitiated. There is a need for effective communication strategies that can distill the essence of AI into clear, concise messages that resonate with the required audience.

8.2. Systemic Integration Problems

Another hurdle that exists is the integration of AI systems into the existing landscape of a telecom company's procedures. Issues such as legacy infrastructure, data silos, and incompatible software systems can cause a project to fail before it begins. Significant investment of time, resources and importantly, a shift in mindset are required to successfully implement AI by replacing or modifying legacy systems.

8.3. Regulatory Hurdles

Telecommunications is a heavily regulated industry. Companies must adhere to domestic and international rules set by various regulatory bodies. These regulations often impact how data is managed and used, which directly affects AI's functioning and its benefits. A thorough understanding of these laws and their potential changes is crucial for the successful implementation of AI in telecommunications.

Moreover, privacy concerns over AI's data collection and usage are mounting. Telecommunications firms have access to massive amounts of personal data, and AI's ability to process this data efficiently can inadvertently lead to privacy breaches. Regulatory compliance and data management in AI applications are complex tasks, and firms will need to devote considerable resources to tackle these challenges.

8.4. Technical Challenges

A substantial technical challenge lies in the form of data management. Telecom companies accumulate massive volumes of data daily. While AI can indeed process this data, it is also contingent on the accuracy and consistency of the said data. Erroneous, low-quality, or inconsistent data can significantly impact AI's output quality, leading to an inaccurate analysis that could be potentially damaging.

Additionally, AI models need to be trained and tested, which requires substantial computational resources. As the complexity and size of models increase, so do computational demands. Consequently, high performance and robust infrastructure is necessary to handle these operations, which in turn ramps up costs.

8.5. Security Concerns

As AI systems continue to embed themselves in our daily lives, the threat of misuse and malicious hacking grows parallelly. AI's potential to 'learn' and 'decide' opens the door for cyber attacks that could compromise user privacy, manipulate data or disrupt critical services.

Overall, while AI holds a bright promise for the telecommunications industry, these obstacles must be recognized and addressed strategically. The aforementioned challenges and dynamics suggest that the journey to a fully AI-integrated telecom sector is intricate, demanding concerted efforts on multiple fronts—from fostering an AI-literate workforce and upgrading legacy systems to honing a laser-sharp focus on privacy, regulation and security concerns.

Chapter 9. AI and the Future of Telecommunications

As we stand at the precipice of a digital revolution, AI's role in telecommunications seems destined to grow, setting the stage for a future where high-speed, efficient, and personalized telecom services become the norm. All aspects, from the network infrastructure to customer service and predictive maintenance, stand to benefit from this fusion of technologies.

9.1. AI - A Game Changer for Telecom Infrastructure

The telecommunication industry's backbone consists of a complex array of systems and infrastructure. The uninterrupted flow of information hinges on the seamless functioning of these components. In this context, AI can prove to be transformational, augmenting both the reliability and efficiency of telecom operations.

Through Machine Learning (ML) and Deep Learning (DL) algorithms, AI can aid in smart routing of data packets. It can analyze the most efficient path based on a variety of factors such as network traffic, distance, and device type. It effectively mitigates the risk of bottlenecks, ensuring uninterrupted service delivery and enhanced user experience.

Moreover, AI algorithms can predict possible infrastructure failures by constant monitoring and analysis of system health. Such predictive maintenance allows for timely action, pre-empting system failures and significantly reducing downtime.

Chapter 10. Unleashing the Power of Cognitive Computing

As an advanced subset of AI, cognitive computing is pushing the boundaries of what's possible in telecommunications. These systems mimic human cognitive abilities to learn, reason, and engage, opening new avenues for telecom players.

This includes creating dynamic pricing models, auto-detecting fraudulent activities, and even enhancing cybersecurity measures. Advanced neural networks, a significant component of cognitive computing, can detect anomalies and potential threats, flagging them for human intervention.

10.1. Personalized Customer Service - The Way Forward

Another revolutionary application of AI in telecommunications is the promise of personalized customer service. Telecom companies handle colossal amounts of data every day, and harnessing AI can help make sense of these vast data pools. It can revolutionise how telecom service providers understand and engage with customers.

AI systems can correlate multitude customer data to generate insightful predictions about customer behavior. Telecom companies can use these insights to create tailored recommendations and personalized service packages.

Additionally, AI-backed chatbots and virtual assistants are becoming invaluable tools for providing 24/7 customer service. They can handle several customer queries simultaneously and in real-time, leading to quicker resolution and improved customer satisfaction.

10.2. Network Optimization through AI

In the face of growing network complexity, service providers often grapple with provisioning and management of network resources. AI can help develop flexible, self-optimising networks that can adapt based on real-time demands. Algorithms can study patterns in network load, identify peak times, and even predict future network congestion, allowing for effective load balancing and resource allocation.

Moreover, AI, through predictive analytics, can forecast network expansion needs based on current trends and growth projections. Telecom operators can leverage this data for informed decision-making regarding network upgrades, expansions, or launching new services.

10.3. Concluding Thoughts: AI and the Telecom Future

As we delve into AI's potential within telecommunications, we uncover a boundless cosmos of opportunities. AI is not just an enabling technology, but an accelerator of innovation, capable of reinventing the industry's future landscape.

Of course, the road to this AI-powered telecom future isn't devoid of challenges that include ensuring data privacy, handling algorithmic bias, and the need for sizable investments in AI technologies. However, with careful policy-making, regulatory compliance and strategic planning, AI's benefits undoubtedly outweigh these hurdles.

This transformative twin-powered relationship between AI and

Telecom will undoubtedly usher in an era characterized by efficiency, personalization, and improved network reliability. It presents a future where our dependence on telecommunications for work, play, and everything in between, will be underpinned by the enigmatic, yet empowering realm of Artificial Intelligence.

Chapter 11. Ethical Considerations in AI Implementation

AI implementation in any field, including telecommunications, is never bereft of potential ethical considerations. These considerations often range from issues revolving around algorithmic fairness to data privacy and security, and even to workforce implications. While AI has a transformative potential for reshaping various aspects of telecommunications, it is indispensable to tackle these ethical arenas with due diligence and accountability to ensure a responsible AI ecosystem within the telecom industry.

11.1. Algorithmic Fairness and Bias

AI tools usually learn from data, and any bias inherent in this data can be translated into the AI system's decisions and actions. Within the telecommunications sphere, areas such as customer service, network management, and product recommendations could inadvertently promote inequality if these biases are not meticulously identified and mitigated.

Bias can enter AI systems unintentionally at several stages of its life cycle. It could be during data collection, due to skewed samples, or during model training, due to biases on the part of the designers themselves.

To tackle this possibility, AI systems designed for telecom services should be based on the principles of fairness, which means treating all users equally without any discrimination. To ensure fairness, the testing and auditing of AI algorithms should be a routine process. There should also be transparency in how decisions are made by AI, allowing for the potential to challenge and correct biased outcomes.

11.2. Data Privacy and Security

An inevitable reality of using AI in the telecom industry is the vast amount of data it requires. AI relies heavily on data to learn, improve, and make accurate decisions. This puts forth significant challenges regarding data privacy and security. It's crucial that customers' personal and sensitive data are treated with utmost respect and stringent measures are in place to secure that data from potential misuses or breaches.

When implementing AI, telecom companies should adhere to privacy by design principles. This implies incorporating privacy elements from the outset of the AI system's design phase. Furthermore, compliance with global privacy regulations, such as GDPR within the EU, plays a significant role in the responsible handling of user data.

11.3. Workforce Implications

As with any technology-driven transformation, the integration of AI comes with significant implications for the workforce. If AI systems take over tasks typically performed by human employees, it's crucial to consider the societal implications of potential job redundancies and the need for re-skilling.

To mitigate such negative impacts, telecom companies could foster a nurturing environment where their employees are equipped with the necessary skills to work alongside AI. They could also explore how AI could aid in job enhancement, rather than job replacement, by automating tedious tasks and freeing up staff to focus on more value-added roles.

11.4. Trustworthiness and Transparency

Trust is a cornerstone in the interaction between AI systems and their human users. For this trust to evolve, transparency becomes paramount, enabling users to know and understand how AI makes decisions that may impact them. Transparent AI refers to algorithms that operate in a manner that is explainable and understandable to humans.

In the context of the telecom sector, AI applications such as personalized advertising or automated customer service need to balance between user personalization and respecting their autonomy. Telecom companies should thus aim for their AI to be "explainable by design", ensuring their customers understand their interactions with AI, making AI a trusted partner rather than an opaque and misunderstood algorithm.

11.5. Liability and Accountability

Another essential ethical consideration is understanding who should be held accountable if an AI system makes a mistake, especially one that may have serious implications. Given that AI systems are typically complex and multi-layered, establishing accountability might not be straightforward.

Within the telecom industry, accountability should lie with the organizations deploying AI, demanding the adoption of robust monitoring and auditing practices to ensure their AI systems function as intended and are under continual review to prevent undesirable outcomes.

To sum up, ethics should be placed at the heart of AI adoption in telecommunications. By doing so, the industry can navigate these complexities responsibly and build an AI-driven landscape that respects user rights, fosters trust, and enhances overall societal well-being. It's worth noting that the ethical considerations discussed above are not exhaustive, and as AI evolves, new ethical quandaries will likely emerge. Therefore, adaptive and ongoing ethical strategies should be woven into the fabric of all AI implementations in telecommunication, keeping in stride with the dynamic nature of AI and its intricacies.

Chapter 12. Nurturing an AI-Ready Workforce in Telecommunications

In the ecosystem of telecommunications, one significant prerequisite for the evolution of AI is fostering an AI-ready workforce. This endeavor requires holistic changes encompassing education, training, and fostering a culture of innovation where AI thrives. This change isn't for the distant future; it is required now.

12.1. Education and Training

Education and training form the backbone of initiating any kind of technological evolution, including establishing a workforce ready for AI. To begin with, telecom operators must concentrate on creating a curriculum that embraces the AI realm — from basic principles to their application in telecommunications scenarios.

Yet, for education and training to be effective, they cannot be presented as separate concepts. Instead, they should be deeply entwined in the ever-changing landscape of a worker's tasks. This doesn't mean replacing human judgement, but rather enhancing it. By interacting with AI systems, employees can learn continuously from the feedback the technology provides, fostering adaptation to the AI-powered environment. This adaptive learning approach should undoubtedly become a fixture in all organizations.

Moreover, training shouldn't be a one-shot process but continuous and evolving, molding itself with the evolution in AI technologies. The skills to be enhanced can range from specific programming languages such as Python, R, C++, Java which are extensively used in AI applications, to getting familiar with APIs of common AI service providers.

12.2. Psychological Readiness

Preparing for the AI revolution isn't just about technical skills. It's critical to cultivate a psychological readiness towards this shift. Change management, therefore, plays a pivotal role in this aspect. Telecom companies must work on strategies that help employees gradually adapt to AI systems, minimizing the shock of the change and maximizing acceptance.

To accomplish this, telecom companies can take small steps such as incorporating AI in day-to-day processes gradually and explaining to their employees how AI can make their roles more efficient. By encouraging a seeping integration of AI rather than a sudden implementation, employees can slowly start trusting the technology.

Also, organizations can design supportive measures to alleviate the fear of job loss due to AI implementation. Assurances of job reskilling or redeployment can help employees see AI as an addition to their work rather than a substitution, thereby fostering positive attitudes.

12.3. Building a Culture of Innovation

Another cornerstone of nurturing an AI-ready workforce is fostering a culture of innovation. Rather than being averse to AI due to fears of complexity, employees should be prompted to embrace it, to experiment with it, and to innovate.

This mindset can begin with leaders, who can demonstrate an exploratory attitude towards AI, inspiring the entire organization. Workshops, brainstorming sessions, or AI-centric innovation programs can also provide forums for employees to express their ideas, encouraging them to be a part of the AI transformation rather than just passive recipients of it.

12.4. New Roles and Responsibilities

With the advent of AI in the telecom landscape, the roles and responsibilities within telecom companies are bound to change. Fresh roles may emerge, old ones may get redeployed or redefined — but all roles will be impacted.

For instance, customer service representatives may have to deal with AI chatbots taking over their roles partially, requiring them to migrate to tasks that chatbots can't handle. Similarly, AI could help network administrators by automating functions like load management, root cause analysis etc., allowing the latter to focus on strategic issues.

Amid these AI-induced job changes and redefinitions, it's crucial to have transparent communication. The clear portrayal of the function of AI, the benefits it brings, and the changes it entails will make employees ready to cope and welcome the AI-ready future.

12.5. Exploring Collaboration and Partnerships

With AI being a relatively new terrain, numerous telecom companies may lack the internal expertise to train their employees. To address this, collaborations and partnerships with educational institutions, tech firms, and AI startups can prove extremely beneficial.

Such collaborations can bolster the organization's AI competence, offering general as well as specific training programs. They can also aid in staying updated with the latest AI technologies, thereby equipping the telecom workforce to operate cutting-edge technologies effectively. This will also uncover unseen opportunities and avenues that can be capitalized on.

While the path to nurturing an AI-ready workforce in

telecommunications may seem laden with challenges, the rewards it promises are more significant. Its impact spans the entire scope of operations while also promising an extraordinary potential for growth, profitability, and customer satisfaction. Therefore, forward-thinking telecom companies should waste no time in embracing AI, fostering an employee culture that thrives with it, and preparing themselves to stay competitive in the dynamic telecommunications future.

www.ingramcontent.com/pod-product-compliance
Lightning Source LLC
Chambersburg PA
CBHW062311290526
45794CB00006B/2757